AF364915

FAULT LINES

CLARISSA SOFÍA

FAULT LINES: A Collection of Contemporary Poetry and Photography

'For Justin Vernon' on pages 29 & 30 contain quoted lyrics:

Re: Stacks
Words & Music by Justin Vernon
© Copyright 2008 April Base Publishing.
Kobalt Music Publishing Ltd.
All Rights Reserved. International Copyright Secured.
Used by permission of Hal Leonard Europe Limited.

The Wolves (Act I and II)
Words & Music by Justin Vernon
© Copyright 2008 April Base Publishing.
Kobalt Music Publishing Ltd.
All Rights Reserved. International Copyright Secured.
Used by permission of Hal Leonard Europe Limited.

Towers
Words & Music by Justin Vernon
© Copyright 2011 April Base Publishing.
Kobalt Music Publishing Ltd.
All Rights Reserved. International Copyright Secured.
Used by permission of Hal Leonard Europe Limited.

Contributing Editors: Jen Campbell, Scarlett Ward

Photography © 2020 Clarissa Sofía

ISBN: 9788409177660

First published in Spain by Clarissa Sofía 2020

www.clarissasofia.com

CONTENTS

FAULT LINE: a break or fracture that occurs when the Earth's tectonic plates move or shift - an area where an earthquake is likely to occur.

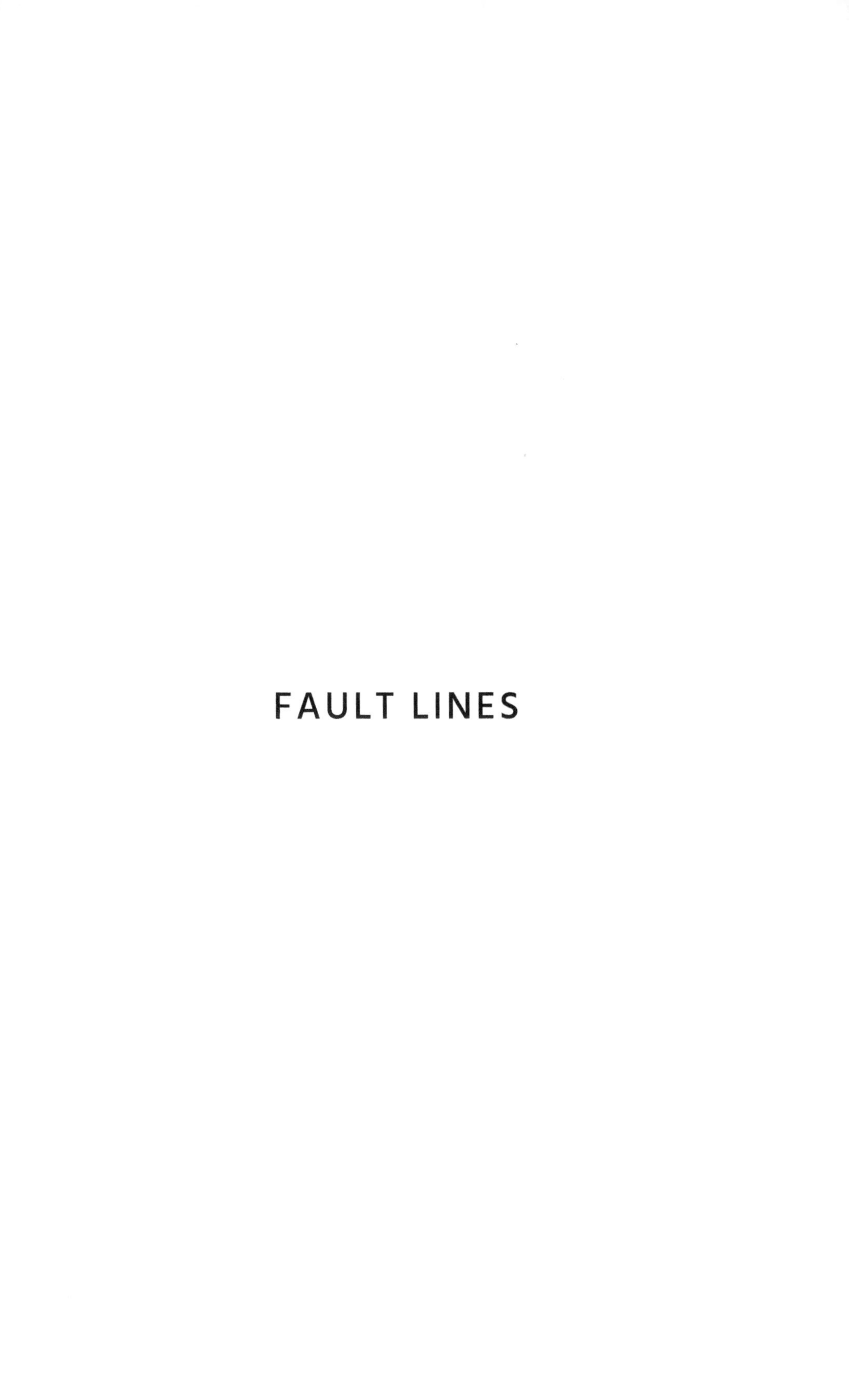

FAULT LINES

CYAN

If I go missing

don't reach me before I have burnt,

I have been people watching

from a pile of ash,

scarcely existing

as I try to figure out which threads to pull.

So I pull all at once,

orchestrate a knot out of feeble remnants,

perversely in control of this mess:

I am everything wrong with me.

If I go missing

don't come looking for me,

the rooftop calls my name more beautifully

than you ever could,

the eyes of 700 tower blocks

staring right at me.

I am as empty as the stars

bruising under a collapsing sky,

barely breathing.

My stomach is full of half woven cobwebs,

dust so grossly present it feeds on me.

If I go missing

don't miss me,

the earth has already grieved for too long,

made peace with the pieces I have left.
But you, you
can still taste the blue dripping through me,
can't seem to rid the aching paste
that has coated your tongue.
You still find residues of my breath
drying out your throat.

If I go missing
don't try to save me,

my limbs have turned to chalk,
crumbled against the groove in your thumb.
And I have already played out
every possible ending:
sickly savoured the sound of lead
scratching letters into your skin,
savoured the final moments of sky fall
before my body greets the concrete.

If I go missing
I am already gone.

BREATHLESS

I found a battered photograph hidden
between the pages of my Grandmother's gold trim bible,

grey and dusty beneath the words of an apostle
I've never read about, coincidently named John.

The picture has been torn in three places
but I can see the glisten of the tape she's used

to bind it back together, to make his face
whole again. He's in black and white

but I imagine his eyes are a celestial blue:
the kind that are soft and welcoming,

the kind that have seen a lot of pain yet choose
to feel the drops on his skin when it rains.

He's smiling profoundly, so big
I can't tell if he's actually laughing.

I wonder what possessed him with joy in that moment,
did someone make a terrible joke? Or was it because

she was smiling at him from behind the camera
because they had the kind of love

that makes you giddy? I wonder what she feels
when she looks at this version of him

trapped inside this worn page,

how many times a day she caresses his face.

It's curious how death sneaks up on us,

snatches our lungs away and leaves us breathless.

I tuck the photo back between the pages,

wonder if he'll see light again, wonder

if he still lingers somewhere or if he simply

doesn't exist anymore. I close the book,

feel the textured cover between my hands,

wonder what it's like to not be anymore.

CYAN CITY

Cyan city,
bulletproof dusk city:
your glass bones
tower above us
looking down
through sombre smog,

buried foundations
decaying
under flower beds
laid pretty.

Ageing city,
romance stained red city:
your walls are built
with artist's hands,
painted by the footsteps
of foreign lovers,

numbing whispers
crisp in British air
turning our hearts
purple and gritty.

Novel city,
mirror crowned aweless city:
ambitious youth
dreamt these streets,
carved new paths

from unwritten poetry,

voices unborn
ferment in feminist bodies
with ideas that wilt
without common history.

Polar city,
concrete clustered steel city:
inherent greed
is burning you from within,
your pavements are grey
and your skyscrapers lonely,

past encounters lost
between hand-me-down skin
and factories bathing
in their own sin.

Cobalt city,
my love for you
is wearing thin.

Our eyes cross paths
for a fraction of a second,
didn't quite have time
to map out all the creases in his face.
I look down at the words
spread across the page like almond butter,

stitching them together in my mind
but they keep unravelling
into a pile of irrelevant clutter.
I look up at the clock:
it's 21:05,
my eyes awkwardly catch his introvert stare –

that looked like a cluster of freckles
below his left brow,
or maybe it was a scar
disguised as caressing constellations.
I'm distracted from my marzipan word stream,
lost interest in my poetic analogies,

just noticed his masculine jaw
beautifully symmetrical and clean –
I wonder if his lips are soft
or if his stubble would tenderly scratch
my bitter cheeks.
21:07:

caught him cautiously analysing

my weary hands,
he's tracing my beetroot veins
as they grow anxious and heavy –
does he know
I'm indulging in fantasies?

Our eyes have met
somewhere between the fog
of simmering cities,
held there for more than 3 seconds,
enchanted by the curiosity we both share –
that's definitely a scar

perfectly framing his pretty-boy eyes.
21:13:
he's teasing my growing intrigue,
making me imagine
the kind of conversations we would have:
unforgettable, inevitable.

I'd tell him about my addiction to photography,
how it's like capturing a firefly in a jar
and watching it glow
under the dark blanket we call night:
a living soul slipping in to its artist skin,
my limbs set free of swollen anxieties.

He'd tell me the names
of his favourite melodies,

slip in a smirk,
inviting me to join his secret therapy.
I'd zone out and start to trace
the imperfections in his face,

curious to know how they came to be.
I notice the missing pigment on his upper lip,
maybe dare to take a closer look,
feel his tongue lightly brush against mine
and drift in an unbreakable kiss.
21:20:

his muscular outline has faded,
an empty metal chair left in his place.

Some days I have the guts
to stare at his raging expression,
an expression I will never understand
nor share with him,
I already adopt too much
of his troubled mind.
He's like a sharp
yet silent splinter
dug under my flaking skin:
too deep to retrieve,
too shallow to feel.
There he lies,
softly scratching the nerve endings
of my fickle fingertips,
controlling me
with hollow words
and preaching false accusations
to an empty room.

I crave you
but I don't
crave you.

Inhaling all that you give me
till I can't breathe
nor feel the unwanted havoc
beneath my heels,
exhaling your demons
till they're no longer mine,
till they shrivel out a cracked drainpipe
pretending they had good intentions in mind.

I want you
but I don't
want you.

Your enslaving power calls to me
like a tragic display
of fabricated happiness,
a temporary paradise making love to me.
You drive my taste buds
to a state of euphoric insanity
till I don't know what's real anymore,
till you're swallowing me slow
in a pool of my own self-hate.

I need you,
I don't
need you.

DORMANT BLACK

"Sleep well,"
you say to me,
plant a kiss
on my swollen lips,
close your eyes
hand on my thighs.

"Sleep well,"
I whisper back,
my eyes fixed
on a ceiling fly,
blank in the night
watering eyes.

I feel my body
sinking
four mattresses
under,
calves so sleepy
they almost feel empty,

hips pressing heavy,
sight slowly fleeting
as time skips three lines:

leaves my body feeling,
mind filling the g a p s ...

                mind

    losing

                                    my mind.

                My chest is thumping:
                heart knocking
                against ribcage,
                pulse throbbing
                like s l o w rain,
            thoughts racing without warning,

                throat closing on free pain
                silently choking the fever,
                I'm rising out of my body

                like a lucid dreamer.

                Sounds smack my cheek
                like hail against my teeth,
                waking the dormant black
                hidden beneath the sheets.

                No going back.

FEBRUARY

Have you ever had a reoccurring dream?
It is always February in mine.
A woman with a gold claw for a tongue
vomits my name into the river –

it is always February. In mine
all the noise is turning white,
she vomits my name into the river –
I am paralysed and she is

all the noise turning white.
Her mouth opens wide and swallows the night,
I am paralysed. She sheds
her barbed wire skin in my bed,

her mouth opens wide and swallows the night:
night morphs into melancholy melts into me,
her barbed wire skin in my bed.
Thorns of a ghost coil and

white morphs into melancholy melts into me,
the taste of iron is colder than I imagined it to be.
Thorns of a ghost coil and
pierce my lips red,

the taste of iron is colder than I imagined it to be.
A woman with a gold claw for a tongue
dissolves into tar and the river turns black,
and it is still February.

WAKE UP

Wake up my love,

Nostalgia grasps you with its deathly hug, you
give yourself in, fall asleep in its glass arms.
Spoiled mist has swarmed Highgate and you can't see
the sun grows lonely, desperate for the touch of your skin.

Can't you see her? Mother is fading,
curdled affection is spilling out of her mouth,
her wasted words struggling to hold back the tears
as she clings to fleeting traces of you.

Wake up my love,

wake up before the world is dead.

Sister is stitching your name across her ribcage:
eight letters long, eight chances for you to finally see
it's her most beautiful work to date, but your view
is refracted 45 degrees backwards.

They've flipped the black switch

and brother's stopped calling,
he's tired of watching you pick away at velcro-lined
promises, pacing at arm's reach
while you slumber in the depths of a stagnant heart.

Wake up my love,

The fog is spreading across your glass bed,
barely left space for the curves of your legs –
loose fixtures hang absently as the last sparks
of electricity reach a thousand dead ends.

These glass arms: a vacant haze of stale air,

FIND ME

Please don't pity me.

If I Let you in on a secret

maybE this will be painless for the both of us:

my hands pAint the letters that my lips struggle to spell –

D   E   A   T   H

Smothers me in every kind of dream,

Erases time from my memories –

all the Foul parts of being.

Did I speak too honestly? Don't worry,

I'll push those words Neatly back down my throat,

it was merely a fleeting Demon,

stopped by for fresh Mint tea.

DoEs he visit you too?

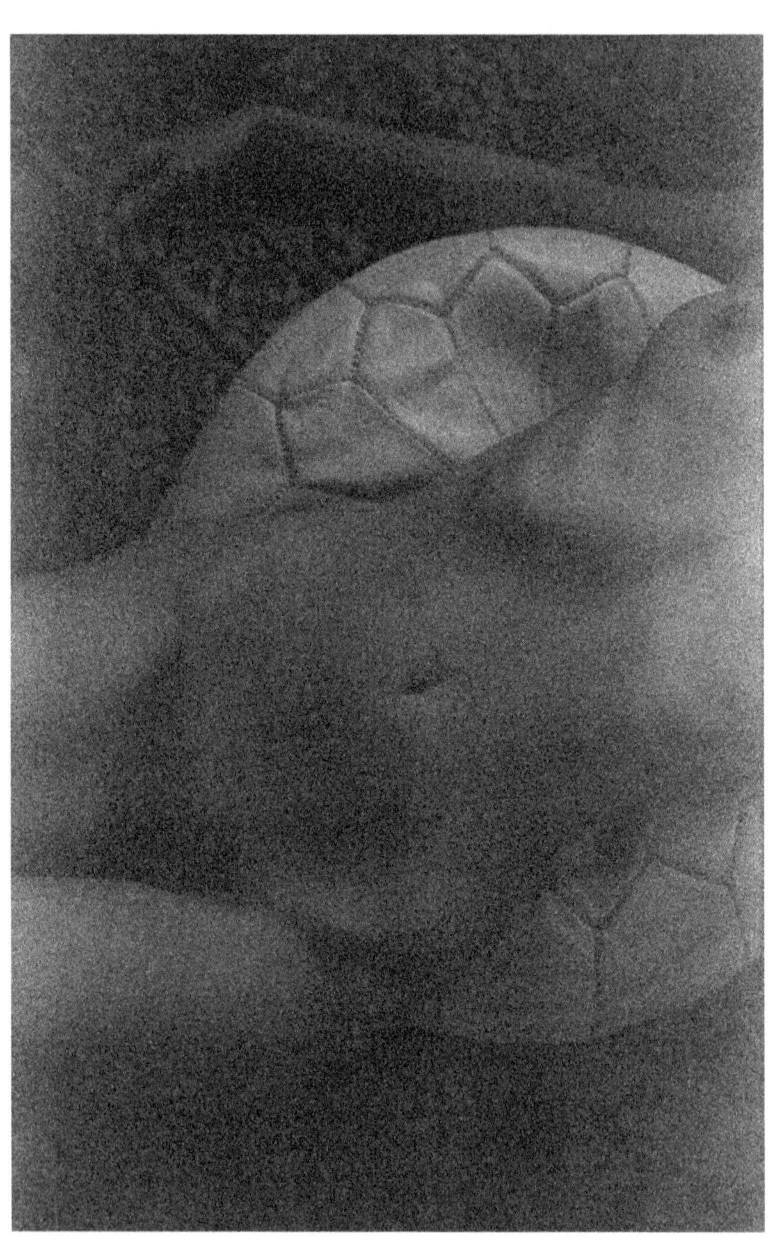

Someone once told me I shouldn't listen to 'sad' music,
that it would only make me feel worse.
But they didn't understand how warm it felt
to have the emptiness kicked out of you,
to have sadness crawl in
to all of your hollow spaces.

Your lyrics clung to my hands
when my arms were too skeletal to make the first reach,
your pain a friend

'when my eyes were all painted in Sinatra blue',

a hiding place I could mould into
when the rest of the world was fast asleep.

You were my relief
when I was searching for seventeen,
unaware that I wasn't the only one.
I felt every note travel through me,
burning my flesh the way a cigarette smokes a body
from the inside out.

You made life tangible,
turned it into bite-sized moments that were malleable,
your voice a sedative when it was all too much
and a caffeine shot when it wasn't enough.
You were my pillow to cry on
after an endless day of wearing a counterfeit smile,

the mattress that would break my fall
as the heaviness of the night crumbled my back.
You were my walk through the park
when everything around me dissipated into white noise,
when it was too dark outside
to see past the Weeping Willows.

You sat next to me on a century-old bench,
watching an image of me
stepping in to the winter pond,
imagining the sharpness of the icy water
climbing from my ankles to my teeth
before it lulled into numbness.

'This is pouring rain,
this is paralyzed',

the Ornamental Grass soaring over me,
wondering if you ever felt this too
'in the towers of your honeycomb'.

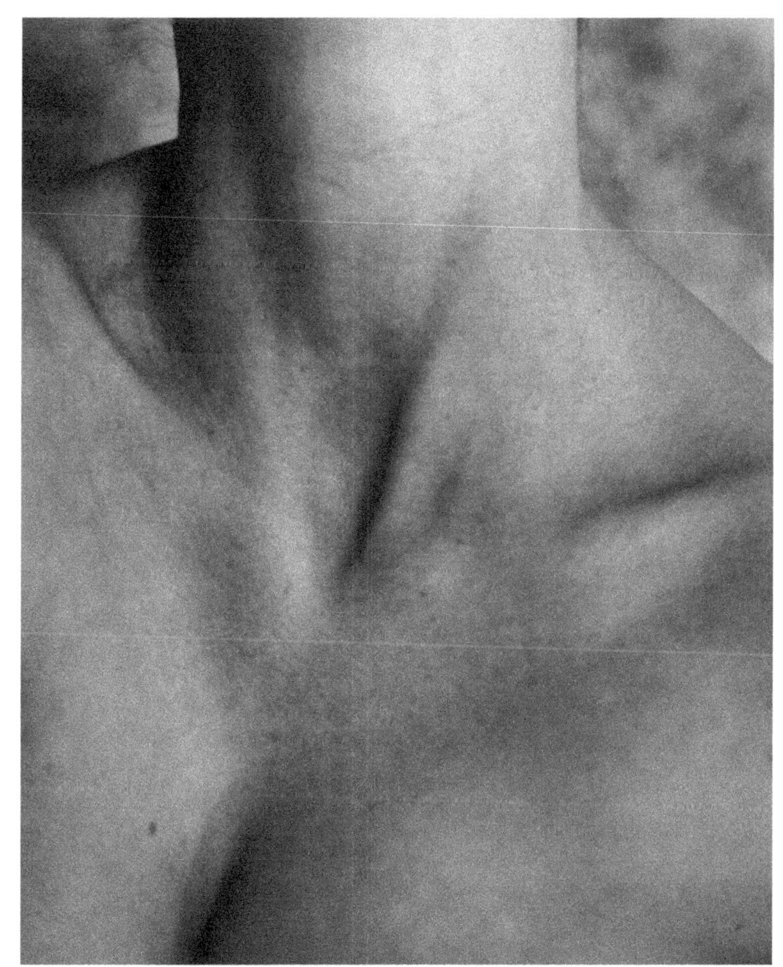

Somewhere between prepubescent crimson and the opening tokes of adolescence, I lost myself. Between howling winter gasps on Primrose Hill and the sleepless nights chasing after London's promised pavements, I lost myself. Somewhere between my undoing and my becoming, I met you. You showed me my reflection in the bleak English puddles, taught me how to re-carve the dent in my cheekbones. Sometimes I'd stare at you while you drifted off into your sleep, you always looked so peaceful, so mellow. You had this habit of exhaling all of your willingness onto my face, breath by breath, I'd listen to the sound of its rhythmic patterns caressing my pores as you slipped away into the night – you only belonged to your dreams now. I was still in my self-inflicted habit of collecting teardrops in ashtrays, and every night, that carved reflection we drew together would sink away with you. I was left to my ever slowing crave for ache. For those few hours, I would project a new world: one without your touch, without your sweet and soulful words to make me feel something more than the emptiness that lingered inside me. I still hadn't figured out which reality scared me more: the one where you showed me who I could be, or the one where I would stay, motionless in all those in-betweens.

SCARLET

BORDERLINE

Close to the borderline | of distance
I found pastel horizons
placid like the ideal mind,
only in reach to the woman
who can walk on waters combined.

Close to the borderline | of doubt
I slid under hibernating fog,
absently shrinking into oceanic blue,
unaware that I was filling your sunflower vase
with enraptured dew.

Close to the borderline | of nothing
I fell into an empty well,
flooded it with my own self-pity
and floated amongst declining memories;
only finding reason in limestone reflections.

Close to the borderline | of you
I decorated my pit with cut out daffodils
and cherry painted windmills,
my smile was as silver as seaside dusk
and your soul was as gold as an ivory tusk.

Close to the borderline | of love
I felt your touch deep between my breasts,
your words buried into my chest
and built their residence into a silk nest.

You used to live
a life without love,

without blushing cheeks
and wild-eyed cries,
filtered coffee kisses
addictive like nicotine.

We used to miss without knowing
we were missing:

9 PM encounters by
seaside margins of youth,
adolescent blues
escaping out fluorescent fingertips,

draining our hands
till our skin melted
like candlesticks.
I used to desire a connection
stronger than the ink
between the browning pages

of childish play scripts, stacks of books
forming fortresses of nothingness.
Emptied knowledge
spilt from unread novels
poetically framing my almost womanly body,
rosy pink and swelling like mulberry.

We used to miss without knowing
we were missing:

11 PM strolls
down starlit dirt roads,
bruised with temptations
of our wildest reflections,
inevitably cheating
our parents best lessons.

You used to yearn
to share love stained duvets,
tracing metaphors
round my scarlet lips,
speaking under the afterglow
on a stolen rouge pedalo.

We used to miss without knowing
we were missing:

3 AM embraces
sinking into heated grains
of sinfully witnessed sand,
your cold skin finding refuge
between my hairless thighs –
our escape from painted boundaries,

silent beneath island palm trees.
Sweetened teardrops

engraved like tattoos on your chest,

intricate like an artist's mind

you whispered into my corduroy ears:

"we were missing until we were found."

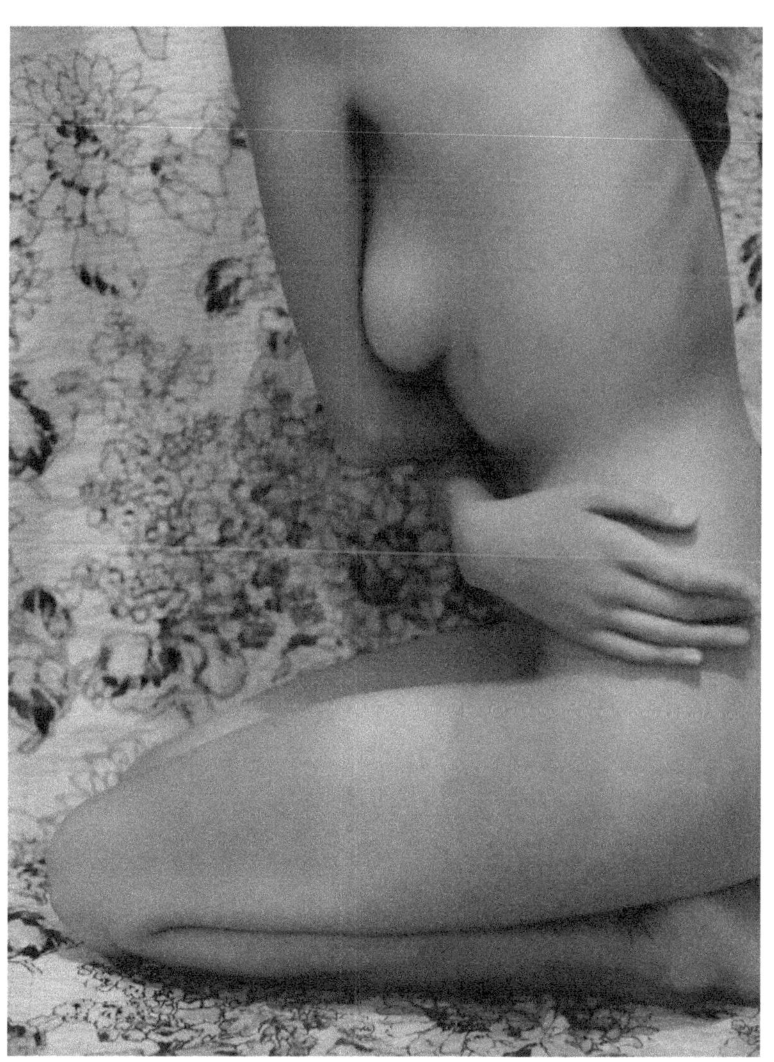

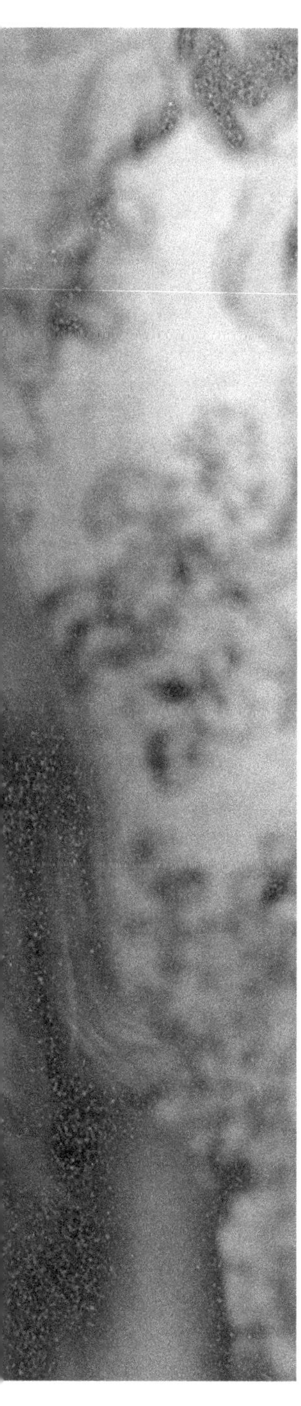

SILENT SCREAMS

I was so in love

with the way

he would passionately

lose himself

in his own melodies,

yet so bored

watching him.

Watching him

press down

on those keys

as their hypnotizing notes

hollowed   out

the sounds

of my silent screams.

THE FLAW IN OUR TONGUES

Our hearts are kept at a distance
by the flaw in our tongues.

You speak in southern rhymes, proud amber toasted
like the arches of the Catedral de Sevilla.

I speak in broken   lines, soft and unsure,
English weather wedged between my vocal cords:

they snap under the weight of your breath
thickening with every exhale,

blurring the yellow smog in the rays of day
and at my relief, thinning under the navy

of night. It is only then that our hearts inch
a little closer, where our words find

a common ground to plant their feet on.
You sing me a poem in flamenco chants,

replace the distance with negative space.
I reply with a half

—attempt at song, my words too slurred
to pronounce the verbs. For a moment we speak

our own language, only drunk candles
between us as our saliva begs us to hold on.

But we both know how slippery it is, and so
we find comfort in collecting silences,

but they've started spilling out and I'm afraid
we won't know what to do with them.

I count the days that pass without seeing you,
a month goes by and I figure my heart

should begin the missing, but it never does.
You call me with what I can only imagine

is the same kind of guilt infested itch –
you speak in father tongue, and I in turn

reply in the role of daughter, the distance
once again loudly pronouncing itself.

PLATONIC LOVE

Your friendship was a turning point
in my adolescence.
First joints by Camden Lock
marked a new era,
new personalities peeled back the covers.

Lambrini vomit – pink and sticky
camouflaged the fresh scars
embedded across your eyes.
Like clockwork, the cooker read twelve
and I'd wait for you to confess to me.

Midnight monologues sucked the purity
out of my cheeks, cold pavements your stage
on sleeping residential streets:
me, the only face in your audience,
the only one you needed.

Alcohol-induced panic attacks
were your favourite party trick,
second in line to first prize:
making sure I never felt the way you did,
refracting reality like it was water.

Almost suicide notes
scratched crosses across my innocence,
the taste of salted caramel
smelting memories into the safe confines
of Soap and Glory boxes.

You were a realist and me a dreamer,
undoubtable like a platonic romance.
No one but you
could have opened my eyes so aggressively
without hurting a single hair on me.

BEYOND OUR EYES

It was the sex beyond our eyes,
the magnetic stare
between our aching thighs.
You:
embedding promise-filled kisses
into my neck,
captivating me fully
as you bathed in my thirsty soul.
Me:
breathing devoted whispers
atop your naked chest,
staining your mind
with a lust-filled serenity
as our hearts collided at the height
of an impossible electricity.
It was you
enveloped
in all of me.

BECOMING ONE

I don't know how you did it, but you stole my heart so politely I didn't know whether to ask for it back. You had me teething uncontrollably, the way you walked into my arms with a confidence that I had only dreamed of wearing, a touch that projected happiness so loudly you managed to wake the entire town. And I recall you singing into my lips, a song that couldn't have pierced my skin more softly - lyrics of an unfound paradise hesitating to announce their arrival, unsure if we were ready to feel the heat of tangled lovers becoming one with the roots of our throbbing hands.

HOME

I found you
talking through synchronised lungs,
permeating metaphors into meaning
with our salivating tongues.

We could almost create our own dimension,
a copycat of our rotting habitat.

Stones would kiss the hardening skin
on the soles of our feet,
our legs treading intrigued
as they play a flirtatious game of seek and go find.

New cities conceive
new colours,
as if to tempt two fusing souls
to its humming land.

In that moment,
it's as if we found home.

We found it isn't shelter
under an English rooftop
nor beneath a feather duvet
that momentarily warms our lonely thoughts,

it's not the chatter of symbolic characters
conversing through our static TV screens

as our limbs sink into that couch
we wish we hadn't bought.

Home is a pulse that imitates the rhythm
of an unconventional jazz song,
throbbing as it embraces the folds
in our rippling bass,

it's my breath teasing your neck
as my kisses lift the hairs on your chest,
the weight that's growing hot and heavy
as you intertwine your yearning hands

with my feline body.
It's that feeling speeding up our spines
as my moans mimic the sound
of your lips tracing my fault lines.

Home is your heartbeat
dancing next to mine.

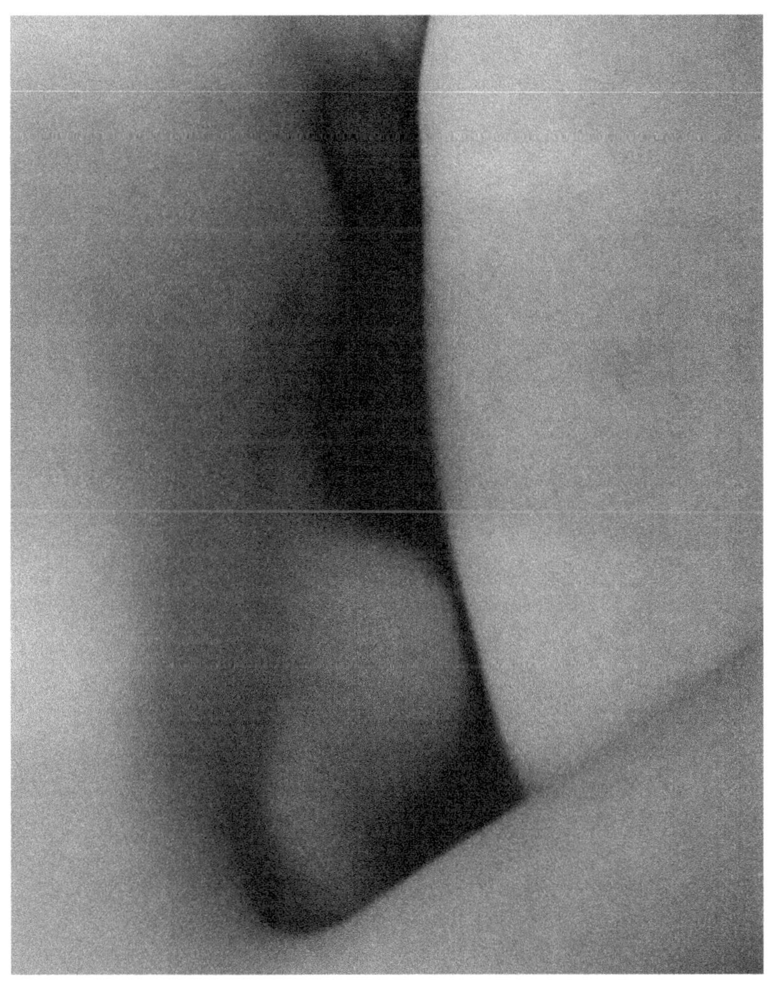

NEON MUSEUM

He looks at me with square eyes.

       I am a neon museum –

doors open for visitors,

mat that reads: 'anyone welcome'

like I'm a tour bus on Oxford Circus,

ticket entry free of charge,

your lucky day they're front row seats.

He smiles at me with lopsided lips

like I'm infatuated by this,

steps asserting his new course,

feet pointed towards my shorts –

       I am a sample rack of leftover denim.

Hands rub his jaw bone

tense like a rusty steel pipe,

he reveals his wonky teeth

like he's something unique.

I smile back

because my mother taught me to be polite

but I keep walking, time is catching up with me.

I feel his thirsty hand on my arm,

almost bruising but not enough to stain.

He speaks with tobacco breath:

"Hey babe, wait up."

like my father chose babe for a name.
I ask him if we've met before,
maybe we know each other from somewhere,
he says no but he thinks I'm cute.

It's a compliment I guess
so I say thanks but I have to go.
He strokes my shoulder then moves down to my waist –
          I am a plastic mannequin in a shop window,
yellow lights flashing above my head: 'Offer ends today!'

"How about a drink?" he spits
"I have a boyfriend," I reply, "but thanks."
He tells me he doesn't mind
like my smile said I want you,
like my eyes said please touch me.

Nerves melt my face
so my smile fades away,
patience a distant state,
I make an excuse and try to get away.
He mutters "slut" under his breath

like I was dressed for his taste.
I've had enough so I push him away,
make my lucky escape –
          I am a graffitied statue
in the centre of the auditorium.

Do you remember that winter day? We were sitting on a damp bench behind Kenwood house and I was staring blankly at the reflection in a muddy puddle ahead of us, you kept asking me what was wrong, waiting patiently for my reply but I never gave you one.

I just kept looking at the way the ripples blew across that puddle, distorting a willow tree until it was undefinable, and all I could think was how freeing that must feel.

But you were digging and pulling and prodding, kept tugging at my brain and I couldn't understand why you wouldn't just leave it alone: the talking and the sharing.
You got sick of hearing me mutter those three words:
"I don't know." It was too late though, you had already planted a hundred questions in my mind that I wasn't prepared to ask myself.

I think deep down you knew that I was begging for someone to keep trying, to keep pulling those words up my throat so they could spill out of me. But they were scratching at my insides so aggressively that I couldn't breathe. My tonsils were bruising and I couldn't find the strength to open my mouth, so I just swallowed them back down and felt that lump cry into me. I forced a smile and said: *"really I'm fine,"* not even fooling myself as a wall of tears barricaded my eyes.

You told me that maybe it was time to say goodbye to us, that you couldn't be with someone who wouldn't even try, you'd already burdened yourself with someone like me before. You had opened yourself up, couldn't understand why I wouldn't give you something back. You were looking at me, trying to find me, so I broke the silence with a pathetic *"OK."* Except it wasn't. And it wasn't the reply either of us wanted to hear me say.

I know we never made it anywhere after that, but I wanted you to know that I will always remember the words you planted in me, the unbroken gazes we shared at Hampstead's edge. It was the first time I dared to look into someone's eyes without looking away because I was too scared they'd be able to see right through me.

You peeled the first layer of guilt off my chest, gently tugged at the fault I was carrying, unknowingly, speaking to me with a mindful sincerity that no one had ever given me.

So thank you for dragging those words halfway up my throat. Because even though you never heard them leave my lips, you taught me that it was OK to give in to the pain of fragmented fists. It was OK to let myself feel, even if it meant losing the battle I had started against myself.

I had been punching down on my own heart, temporarily pleading guilty, I know that now.

Even though you weren't foolproof and I wasn't prepared

for you, your lessons caught up with me. I wanted you to hear
me, finally speaking openly.

Yours Always x

SERENDIPITY

Here we gazed
staring at the endless sunset
from a murky window 300 ft. from limbo,
kayaking in the sky miles above
our thoughts' most comforting cradle.
We were so close

to touching the marshmallow clouds
yet too scared to feel the downpour
of the opportunities that awaited us.
We wandered in the blue of day:
between the harmonising blackbirds
whistling to Lana Del Rey,

sauntered inside the darkness
of the intoxicating night
and buried beneath a duvet
that prickled your porcelain skin.
We never truly soaked
in the warmth of the sun

nor dreamed in the arms of the stars,
we were too blindsided by the beauty
of an unreachable solace,
stuck in a trance of a vision
that we couldn't seem to grasp.
And there we stayed,

until the heat seeped through our enchanted gaze

and burnt a hole through our fragile eyes,
forever yearning to feel the colour
trickle through our fingertips
and down our interlacing spines.

Our black & white hearts
found a field of flowering bodies,
all laid out in rows
of hypnotising poppies and red wine daffodils.
They stood side by side on a sinking ocean floor
and all we could do was watch.

Just as I watched you flee for the oceans,
leaving me and my drowning lens behind,
capturing only the strands of your ash-blonde hair
as I felt you crack our cemented spine.
Here I'll gaze in this sky-born limbo,
out of reach to that fire

we once shared and desired.
So I'll let you find your own ecstasy
and forever cherish the moments
from our most beautiful galaxy,
we'll name it Serendipity.

CINNAMON DREAMS

Take me back to Chiang Mai
where my heart's been left behind,
torn between enchanted memories
and the possibility
of blissful realities.

Dancing by the riverside
spotted Starlings talk to me,
they're riddled with Asian melodies
speaking wide
by interrupted tides.

I long to rest by a humming Teak tree,
admire its acceptance
of the imposing factories,
I'd rinse my sins in coconut waters
where laboured hands
have dented their skin.

How nice it must be
to wake by the weeping Lantanas,
mystical in their unpredictable hue
and gently soothing
under daybreak dew.

I'd watch as translated smiles
travel across fields,
far and distant from city steel,
in search for shaded lemongrass streams;

in search of shaded lemongrass streams

they paint the west

in cinnamon dreams.

INTRUDER

Five hundred and twenty nine-days
I've been able to call mine,
high like summer's first love,
kissing silk willingly against my own flesh.
Did you purposely let me taste joy,

let me savour the sweetness of stability
so when your spite sunk
into the coarse surface of my tongue
I would feel the cut twice as deep?
You've begun planting intruding thoughts

into my daily routine,
begun whispering cheap comments,
accused him of a sheepish personality.
You make me notice his lazy habits
instead of his unravelling talents.

Forty days have faded into eighty yet
I haven't noticed the hands turning,
I've been bathing in the toxic leaves
you hid under my favourite pillow.
Sometimes, I truly believe you've become

a part of me, that you've claimed your home
in the weakest corners of my mind.
Sometimes, your words become mine,
your spiteful actions turn into mine,
your blackness fills mine.

So I let myself drift off for a while,
I let you take control.
I almost drifted too far once,
so far that I couldn't see myself anymore:
I had to paint my face with beetroot pastels

to fill the empty colour in my lips.
But then I met him, and he taught my mind
how to live again. He is the butter
melting between your ghostly hands
and my childlike skin,

the beginning of all my journeys
and the bed I come home to.
He is the taste of certainty in all my poems,
he helps me remind myself
that you are nothing without me.

So I stand on my own two feet,
I brush out the sap you left stuck
between my golden hairs
and I tell you:

you are black.
And I,
I am mother green.

AMBER

SEASONS

Let me take you on a journey.
I'll start at your toes
dug deep under blankets untidily,
they are the backbones of your feet,
connections to the soil
in which you lay your pleats.

Down here in damp darkness
it's hard to feel complete,
your voice too soft to be heard below ten ft.
If they could just loosen this harness,
set you free from this looping thought stream.

Your mind begins to contemplate:
how much time is needed
to claim back your legs from this sinking bed,
run past the nameless faces
guarding this gate?

Maybe it's not about escaping,
maybe it's a trick question,
riddles stretch wider
than the spreading imperfection.
Maybe you need to look deeper,
maybe the exit is beneath your left lung –
take a moment to digest it.

Raspberry dunes reign
like perpetual reflections,

stitched to your stomach
inducing seasonal regression.

You consider the ease of giving in,
letting go of your limbs,
feel the breeze cut your cells
and step out of your skin.

Stop breathing for a moment.
Be weightless like a shadow.
Your veins opaque to the bruising
of a thundering piano,
unstitching plum soaked threads
you're finally able to swallow.

Maybe it's not groundbreaking,
maybe it's as simple as counting,
dreams sticky like maple memories
as vivid as the taste
of your mother's sweet milk.
Maybe it won't be heartbreaking,
maybe the season is changing.

MELANCHOLY MOON

Yesterday I woke

plucking at your sculptured rib cage,

finding traces of a melancholy moon:

my face reflected in its cratered eyes

so I kissed each fold

as you mounted them onto collar dunes.

Today I soaked my hands

in deathless s p a c e,

painting stars around my wilting head:

my mind projected into crescent lips

so you caressed each curve

as I felt us rise out

of our caving worlds.

It's curious how memories sometimes fade, how our brains decide which ones are worth keeping based on our emotions or lack of them. And out of nowhere, doing nothing out of the ordinary, something triggers a feeling in you. Maybe you're watching water droplets fall into your steaming bathtub, and you've seen the way the water ripples like that before, the feeling you had in an almost identical moment to this one. It takes you back to a memory you forgot existed –

takes me back to watching those same ripples

forming in that bathtub

of our home in NW6.

And I remember feeling lost,

like I had to accept something

that I had refused to see.

You had taken too much of me,

and I was just drifting

from dawn to dusk like an empty shell

because you were carrying all of my insides

on your back. Let me rephrase that,

I had given *you* too much of myself.

You never pulled me out forcefully,

I just slid out so naturally

that it only felt right

to let you have all of me.

And I hope you don't mistake that as a bad thing,

because after I had wondered aimlessly

in that hollow shell for too long,

I eventually learnt how to trust.

You were just lovingly taking care of me
till I was ready to carry myself again,
till I could finally wash my own skin
without scrubbing too hard
because those ripples were staring at me,
judging me.

This time with both our hands equally heavy,
we carried each other proudly.
I had forgotten how much that meant to me.

THE TWO SIDES OF ME

I like the left side of my body,
in fact, I adore it.
My flesh clings to me longingly
and above my ribcage, my breast lays full.
A mole sits diagonally above my belly button,
making me feel like there's only one me.

Sometimes I can even feel the life
that grows from my skin
like it's fertile soil
in Balearic spring,
roots make their way into richer tissues
feeding on arborescent cells.

When I look down
I see daisies and almond blossoms,
pines and palms perfectly poised,
all growing out of me
as though gravity weren't there
to weigh them down –

looks like a home for mountain fairies.

Then there is my right side:
sagging and sad as though it didn't belong to me,
how could it when it wilts
next to paradise fields?
It smells of ice-cold winter
but not the cosy kind,

it's empty here.

When I look down all I see
is self-loathing:
a dull surface that moulds at the touch,
stretch marks that sink too deep,
thigh that's a millimetre too wide.
My hipbone sticks out at the wrong angle

so sharp it could cut
those love bearing hands –
the cause of its own agony,
unwanted like no one has ever hugged it,
like no one ever told me I could choose
to equally love both sides of me.

BECOMING

We are unceasingly becoming,
plucking carefully
at these lucid moments,
digesting only what belongs to us.

We collect conversations,
pulling the thoughts of past lovers
into our trusty dictionary,
referencing borrowed words
as our tongues carve new languages.

We strum on nylon chords,
manifesting an everlasting night,
romanticising over the mundane
till the dull blooms into crayon threads.

Tirelessly they weave,
marking another stitch
into our embellished hearts.
Unravel and reroute this skin,
we are fragments of ever-changing art.

My mental state fluctuates
as often as my body weight.
Last week I woke up in a bed of
r
a
i
n
and a bloated stomach
full of empty pain.
I felt like I was
alone
even though he was standing right next to me.
Tomorrow I know I'll feel the warmth of the city air
holding my hand again,
and my hips won't stick out in layers of fat
the way I thought they did.
I never really know if I actually physically change
or if it's just these mindless circles
dictating my state.
Next week my eyes will be bright again,
I'll find myself noticing the moss that grows
between the cracks in the pavement:
even the most primitive life
finds its way to the light.
So I'll draw a map with clumsy hands
and show myself where the light hides
behind the dark clouding my eyes.

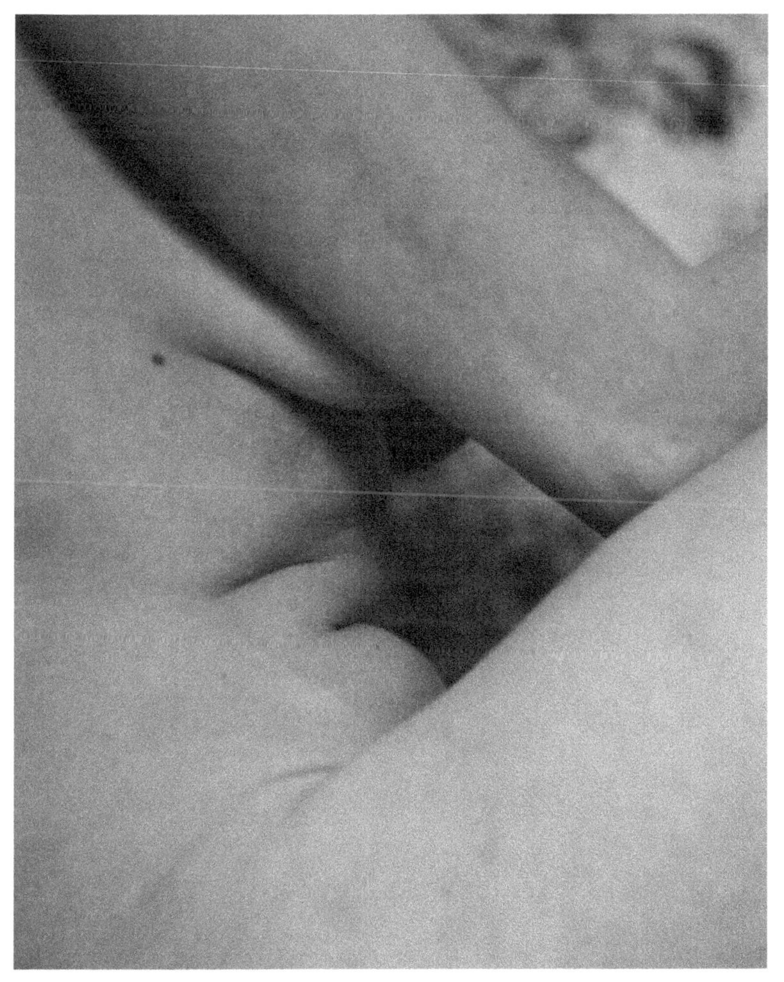

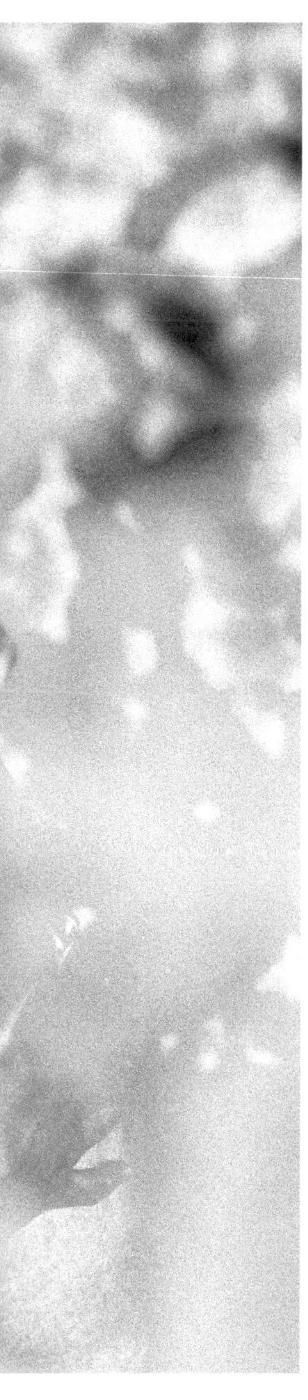

EXISTENCE

Existing in the now has become
a callous chase
I am trapped in,
a predisposition
I am apparently in control of.
Nostalgia tugs at my toes,
entices me with lustful memories
as she replays iridescent films
in front of me.
The absence of tomorrow
is tainted by the longing
marked on my lips,
possibilities pleading
for a chance to be tasted.
I am lingering between the two,
birthing myself
into the present,
brutally living this anomaly.

Too often, we question ourselves. We question what we are doing with our lives, what we want, ponder where we've come from and who we are. The answer is so much simpler than our complex minds would let us believe. I can only try my best to help you see:

You are
the words whispered softly
between sleepy coffee sips,
the split second breaths   between steps
as your body momentarily
rebels against gravity,
the midnight laughter
between tipsy friends
as you stumble through the moonlit streets.
You are every kiss
that has shaped your lips,
every tattered book
that has cradled your brain
and every film that has heard you cry.
You are the smile on a mother's face
as she looks at the reflection
in her child's eyes,
the journeys that you've lived
from fractured homes
to foreign fantasy lands.
You are the soil that feeds the trees,
the bees that make this world go round
and the oxygen that we breathe.

You are a mass of uncountable atoms
each individually alive,
all holding hands as they weave you
into something that resembles human.
You are every person on this earth
all at once, yet still uniquely
and madly

just you.

FAULT LINES

These are my fault lines:
my legs, my hips,
my stomach, my skin,

peach like the colour of sunset sand.
It stretches and tugs and hangs
down from my closet shoulders,
falling like charity shop dresses.

It wraps around my textured spine,
rich like the taste of sweet dandelion wine.
Hugs and warms and sometimes tears
across my hips and tender chest.

Sometimes beauty looks back at me
with watercolour painted symmetry,
reflections cut from a silver cloth,
thighs spread regal in perfect monotony.

Other times disgust possesses me
shifting my sight blindly,
feet drowning in hollow puddles
watching the day sink from colour to grey.

I hold my heartbeat in my hand:
squeeze it and prod it and hurt it,
drown it in cashmere mud
then apologise for the wasted blood.

Feel the beats slow down,
rhythm of an ancient town,
deliberately sinking now,
below me somehow.

I notice the seeds in the soil
cosily snug in the blankets of land,
happy to just be.
How I wish I knew how to be.

Like curtains drawn back on Monday mornings,
they're ready to push through.
So I learn to stop seeing with borrowed eyes
and learn to see what I want to be me.

These are my fault lines:
this my heart,
      my heart,
         my heart.

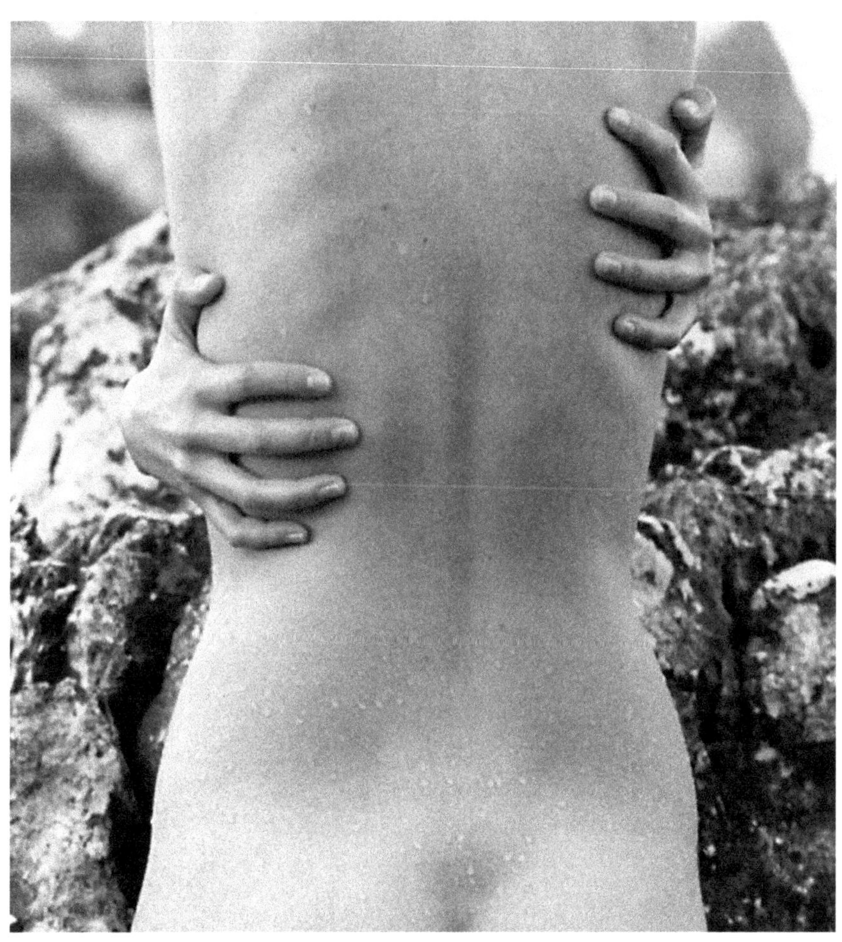

TIME-LAPSE

I was like an undeveloped film roll
hiding in a darkroom shed,
sulking-silver bathing
in my expired innocence.
Overexposed frames still haunt me,
scratching at the nerves behind my eyeballs,
so I watch these textures dissolve
like contrails in the sky
as that silver seeps into my skull.
Salt dunes exfoliate my skin till it bleeds,
till they find my breaking point.
My dreams turn into consolation,
light reborn as the sea baptises me –
this space distorted,
fish-eyed like a pinhole camera,
shapeless like this memory.
A colour image is desaturated
till my vision cries in black and white.

I can't feel her anymore,
she's drained every word out of me,
every shutter pressed –
emptied,
here.

CERTAINTY

I create
because it's the only thing
I know is certain.
Amongst all the chaos and uncertainties
we live through each day,
the flaws we compulsively weigh,
blindly, we question why that girl
can't stomach a meal.

So I sit
and I create.

It's the only way
I know how to express my fears,
because it muffles out
the murder and injustice
I hear about on the news.
Terror is being injected
into us
        as anxiety
and its demons
celebrate another success.

So I create.
Because we are all spoon-fed
a single truth
that we all need to be a certain way.
Because I am a female
and I need to embody

an ideal woman,

paint my face

so that I can look pretty.

So I sit here and I create.

Because my body

is just as beautiful as any,

my skin is as tough as the seas

and as vulnerable

as the words on this very page.

I am just as powerful as the voice

inside each and every one of us.

I create because we have too much to say.

We climb through the mist

of this perfectionist society,

battling with ourselves

      to not get lost

as we do our best to pave our way.

So I create,

because it's the only thing

I know is certain.

SKYLINE

I watch her hang lavender laundry
on a rooftop of a five-storey block,
tangerine clouds l i n g e r i n g
a moment too short.
She pegs the last garment
slightly overlapping
a pair of denim skinny jeans,
then I watch as her sunset silhouette disappears
behind an antenna-lined wall.
No one left
but the declining sky and I.
Remember how that once used to paralyse me whole:

being alone.

But the thing is,
it only feels right now.
The evening lights are waltzing between my eyes,
my lips mouthing love letters
in an amber stained sight:
unapologetically, devotedly,
my reflection is smiling back at me.

UNRAVELLING

Teach me how to breathe this air,
it is tainted with unfamiliarity,

warm and satin as it enters my lungs kindly.
The black I have been carrying

has found an escape route, drained
the excess cortisol from my organs:

now I understand what having weight
lifted off your shoulders truly means.

Teach me how to walk this floor,
I have been treading coal and ice,

adorned myself in thorn stitched cloth.
But I am learning this earth hugs softly,

forgives relentlessly. Teach me
the intricacies that rest beneath my skull,

I am yet to map out the maze I unwittingly
dictated, peel off society's stamp

and rewrite the fallacies. I want to curate
the art on the walls of my mind,

hang up all of my honesties. I am learning
to swim when my tears fill the room,

to dance with sorrow and to pine for tomorrow.
I am unravelling, gradually ripening.

It has been long since I tasted
these honeyed fumes, but I am starting to see

new colours in the spines of the leaves,
I can see the future is alive

as it pulses light through all
the new shades of me.

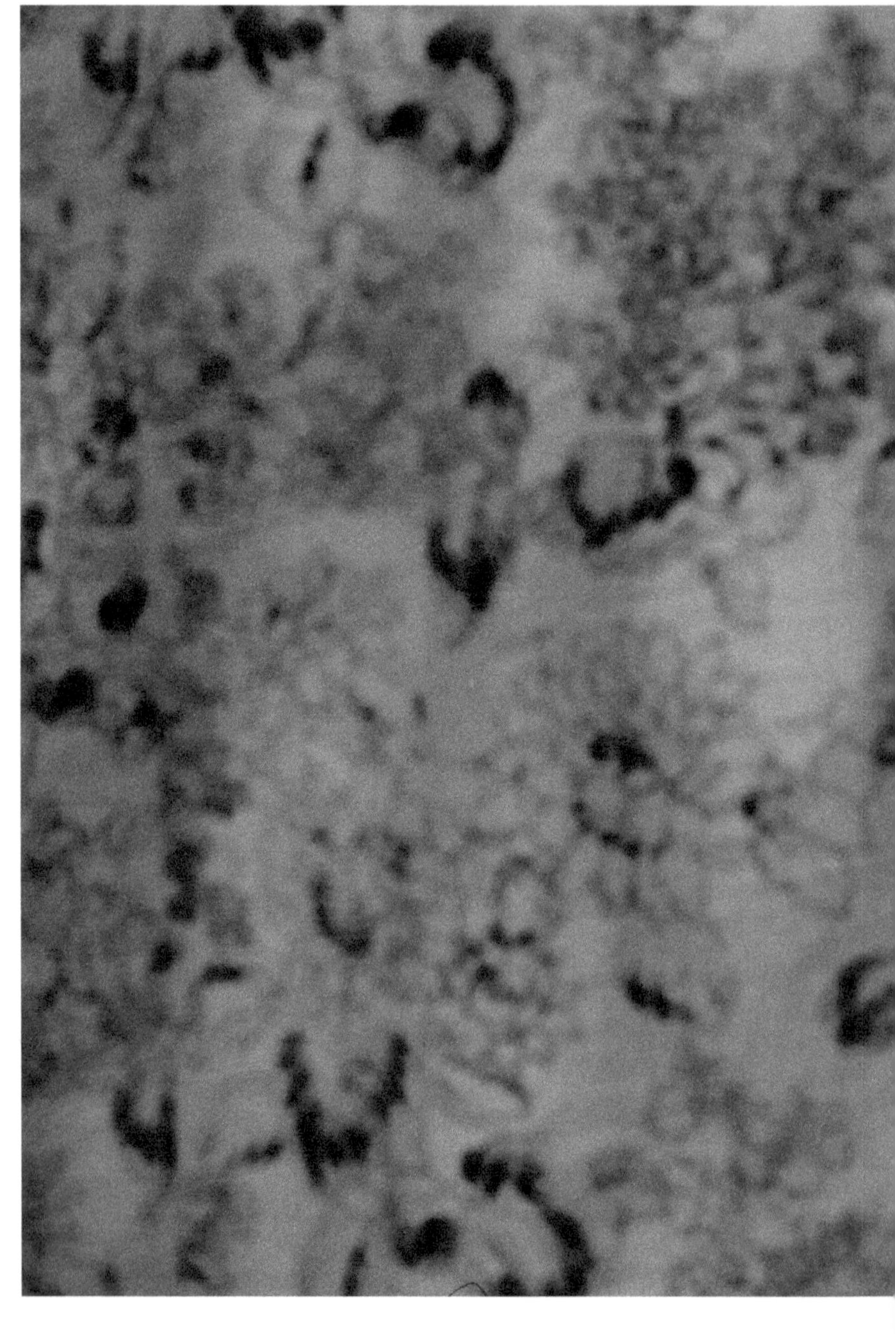

ACKNOWLEDGEMENTS

I want to thank my mother Sophie, for showing me what it means
to be a strong woman.

My sister Romina, for all the love you have put into helping me
with this book. For all the late-night texts and all the advice,
but mostly for being my best friend.

Antonio, for inspiring all of the love poems I've written, for
always being there to lift me up and for bringing out the best
in me.

And lastly, thank you to the unique soul holding this book, for
allowing pieces of me to exist through you.